The Write Feelings

Writing Your Way
to a Better Day!

Kimberlite
Kreations

The Write Feelings

Writing Your Way to a Better Day!

Books in this series:

The Art of Feeling

Paper Feelings

The Write Feelings

ISBN 978-1-947751-34-7

Copyright © 2018 Kimberlite Kreations

KimberliteKreations.com

Introduction

The Concept

Emotions are tricky things... I'd venture to say that most people struggle with their emotions more than any other issue in their life.

"I just want to be happy."

"Oh, that makes me so mad!"

"If only I wasn't discouraged all the time."

"I can't help feeling this way."

As children, we learn pretty quickly how to either use our emotions as a tool to manipulate others or to suppress them so they are not an inconvenience. Oftentimes, we are as much at the mercy of these feelings as everyone else is. They come and go, defying even description. As we grow older, they begin to compound and build on each other so that we feel many different emotions at once, complicating the matter still further. Slowly, fear creeps in. We are being ruled by something unknown to us, but yet intimate to us, the worst kind of enemy.

However... There is Hope at the bottom of Pandora's Box. People are not meant to be merely victims, stumbling through life at the whim of our feelings. The reason our emotions are so difficult is because we don't know how to deal with them. We hardly even know what they are!

That is why books like this can be one of our greatest tools on this journey called life. I don't say it's a weapon to conquer our emotions, because emotions are not meant to be conquered. They're meant to be felt, and they're powerful because they are important. When a woman births a baby, the contractions are not her enemy. They are her own body trying to bring forth her child. They cannot be more powerful than her, because they are her.

The same way, emotions cannot be more powerful than us, because they are us. We don't have to conquer ourselves, we just want to put everything in its proper place so that we can enjoy life instead of dreading it.

So how do we do that?

Practical Application

First, we identify the unknown so it's not so scary anymore. What is our soul feeling? Sometimes the answer is obvious, sometimes it takes a bit of searching. Certain emotions often act as covers for other emotions, and they're surprisingly consistent. There's a book called "Core Lies" by Sarah Mae that I'd recommend for anyone wanting to delve deeper into that subject. For now though, we'll stay simple.

Our first assessment may be, "I feel mad."

But then we ask ourselves the question, "Why do I feel mad?"

Oftentimes, for me at least, the answer is, "Because I am afraid."

For instance...

I have a young child who is more adventurous than my other children. The other day he ran out in the street and almost got run over by a truck. I shouted at him as I snatched him off that street. He thought I was angry. And at first flush, I did feel angry. But why did I feel angry?

Because I was scared. I was afraid of losing him. I was afraid of the hole in my life that would create.

Why would fear lead to anger like that? Why is that actually a common issue with many people?

Let's think about it. Both fear and anger are similarly powerful emotions. They are so mighty that they affect your physical body. They jump-start your adrenaline, which speeds up your heart rate and supercharges your muscles, making you run faster and make quicker decisions. This can be good if... say... your kid is blundering into the street and about to get run over by a truck. It gives you the strength you need to reach him and save his plucky little life.

But sometimes the feelings don't go away after they've accomplished their purpose. Or sometimes they're misguided. Staying on alert for very long is a huge drain on the adrenal system, and anger often morphs into destructive tendencies if it's not channeled properly. After snatching my kid from the street, I breathed in a deep breath and let it out, then explained to him that I sounded angry because I was frightened, and I reiterated why it's very important to be aware of your surroundings. But even after our talk, I still felt jittery and frustrated. Anger and fear were still pumping through my system, even though they were not necessary anymore. Emotions have a powerful place in our life because they are important. But in order for us to have a peaceful life, we have to keep them in their proper place instead of letting them run the show. One of the main ways we keep them from taking over is by correctly putting them in their place when they get unruly.

If I would have had this book, then I would have sat down and done one of the exercises in it. I would have identified my emotions, then processed them on the paper to help redirect myself from raw emotion into a state of understanding and calmness. That would have probably been easier than going out and kicking sticks in the yard. (Though that method certainly worked.)

I'm excited to be a part of this project. Here's to improving our quality of life!

Blessings on your journey,

Jessiqua Wittman
Birth Doula and Gritty Fiction Author

How to Use This Book

This book can be utilized by a wide range of age groups. The only prerequisite is that the person can read and write - expressing himself, or herself, through the outlet of words.

There are two papers per exercise. The first paper is framed with barbed wire - this deals with the negative emotion. The second paper has a more delicate frame on it - this deals with the positive emotion.

When a strong, negative emotion is encountered, turn to a lesson, read the intro at the top of each page, and begin writing about the subject matter.

Now turn the page to the positive exercise. Breath three to five deep breaths. Read the transition on the top of the second paper and complete the writing exercise - transitioning the subject matter, through the writing, from the negative experience to a more positive position.

As you write, project your emotions into the story. Allow the subject to express the emotions you are going through. As the story transitions onto a different path, allow those feelings to wash over you as well.

Feel as the subject in the story feels - ie. allow yourself to rage inside as the storm builds and then allow yourself to calm as the storm in the story calms. Feel your muscles tense and then relax. Sometimes things can be ugly. That's okay. That happens. But don't get stuck there. Feel the yuck, but then let's move on to the beauty. There is more health and strength, love and joy, peace and contentment, waiting for you on the other side.

We send blessings and love your way. May these exercises bring you hope and help you along your journey.

100 NEGATIVE Words

Abandoned	Distressed	Ignored	Restless
Afraid	Distrustful	Indecisive	Ridiculed
Alone	Disturbed	Indifferent	Sad
Angry	Dumb	Insecure	Scared
Annoyed	Duped	Invisible	Scatter Brained
Anxious	Edgy	Irritated	Scorned
Apprehensive	Embarrassed	Isolated	Shamed
Ashamed	Emotional	Jumpy	Shocked
Baffled	Exhausted	Let down	Skeptical
Belittled	Exposed	Lonely	Sorry
Betrayed	Fearful	Lost	Stunned
Bewildered	Fooled	Mad	Stupid
Bitter	Forgotten	Manipulated	Tense
Bored	Frustrated	Misled	Terrified
Cautious	Furious	Misunderstood	Tired
Confused	Grieved	Mocked	Tricked
Controlled	Grouchy	Nauseated	Unhappy
Depressed	Grumpy	Nervous	Unimportant
Desperate	Guarded	Overwhelmed	Unliked
Despised	Guilty	Panicky	Unloved
Detested	Hated	Perplexed	Unsteady
Disappointed	Hateful	Preoccupied	Unwanted
Disheartened	Hopeless	Provoked	Upset
Disoriented	Humiliated	Rejected	Weepy
Disregarded	Hurt	Reluctant	Worried

Concerning the positive words, the ones that are <u>underlined</u> are used in this book. The words in italics, are utilized in The Art of Feeling.

100 Positive Words

Able	Creative	Incredible	Recharged
Accepted	Curious	Informed	Refreshed
Affectionate	Delighted	Insightful	Rejuvenated
Amazed	Determined	Inspired	Relaxed
Amazing	Driven	Intelligent	Relieved
Appreciative	Easy-going	Invincible	Safe
Assertive	Elated	Joyful	Satisfied
At ease	Empowered	Kind	Secure
Awesome	Encouraged	Knowledgeable	Self-assured
Beautiful	Energetic	Light	Smart
Brave	Enlightened	Light-hearted	Spunky
Calm	Enthusiastic	Likable	Strong
Carefree	Excited	Lovable	Super
Cheerful	Focused	Loved	Surprised
Colorful	Free	Motivated	Tender
Comforted	Fulfilled	Needed	Thankful
Comfortable	Fun	Optimistic	Thrilled
Competent	Funny	Over-joyed	Trusting
Complete	Glad	Peaceful	Understood
Composed	Gratified	Playful	Useful
Confident	Happy	Pleased	Vibrant
Constructive	Healthy	Positive	Vigorous
Content	Helpful	Protected	Wanted
Cool	Hopeful	Pumped	Warm
Cozy	In Control	Reassured	Wonderful

INTERNAL WAR

Think of the feelings you are going through right now. Imagine that there is a war going on inside of you. There are Tanks! Soldiers! Cannon Balls!

Describe the battle...

Finish the story on the next page…

Internal War

As the war continues to rage on, a cool, gentle rain begins to fall on the battlefield. All the warriors stop fighting and breathe in a deep breath. Suddenly, they don't feel like fighting anymore. The rain makes them feel

Light-Hearted.

(Describe what happens next.)

DINO BITES

Think of the feelings you are going through right now. Imagine that there is a dinosaur in your backyard. He is having a bad day. He feels just like you do.

Describe what the dinosaur is going through...

Finish the story on the next page...

Dino Bites!

The dinosaur wanders into the woods and sits down on a fallen tree. There is soft, warm moss on the tree that makes a nice, cushion. The sun shines through the trees onto the dinosaur and he begins to feel

Optimistic.

(Describe what happens next.)

THE STORM

Think of the feelings you are going through right now. Imagine that there is storm raging outside. The wind is blasting, hail pelting the ground...

Describe the storm...

Finish the story on the next page...

The Storm

The clouds begin to brighten. The hail stops and the wind settles down. The trees begin to straighten back up and the sky begins to clear. All is becoming

Calm.

(Describe what happens next.)

THE FIRE

Think of the feelings you are going through right now. Imagine that there is a massive fire in the forest. Everything is dry and easily burns.

Describe the destruction...

Finish the story on the next page...

The Fire

Suddenly rain begins to fall and firemen arrive. The fire is coming under control. As the firemen slowly get the last of the fire put out, the animals begin to come back to their homes. They see the firemen close by and are

Curious.

(Describe what happens next.)

WRECKING BALL

Think of the feelings you are going through right now. Imagine a wrecking ball. It is swinging back and forth, destroying everything it impacts.

Describe what's happening...

Finish the story on the next page…

Wrecking Ball

As the wrecking ball swings around, it makes its final blow. A man pulls the lever and stops the ball's destructive path. Soon, a construction crew arrives and begins to clean up the mess. As they work, they are feeling

Useful.

(Describe what happens next.)

BROKEN GLASS

Think of the feelings you are going through right now. Imagine looking out a window that is made of broken glass - that window feels like you do.

Describe the window...

Finish the story on the next page...

Broken Glass

The sun begins to land on the glass and it gets very hot. Soon the pieces begin to melt together, forming a solid clear window once more. The glass feels so

Complete.

(Describe what happens next.)

GONE FISHING

Think of the feelings you are going through right now. Imagine a little fish in a great, big lake. It is swimming for its life as other things are trying to eat it.

Describe what is happening...

Finish the story on the next page…

Gone Fishing

The little fish swims this way and that way! Finally, the fish sees a small opening in a log. It swims into the log and finds a little room where nothing can get to it. The fish is no longer running, it now feels

Protected.

(Describe what happens next.)

THE MAILBOX

Think of the feelings you are going through right now. Susie can relate. She got a letter in the mail today. The letter really hit her hard.

Describe what Susie is going through...

Finish the story on the next page…

The Mailbox

Susie decided to go back out to the mailbox to see if there was any more news for her. As she opened her mailbox, a beautiful dragonfly flew out of it. The dragonfly was so colorful that Susie wanted to draw a picture of it. She felt

Inspired.

(Describe what happens next.)

TURBULENT WATERS

Think of the feelings you are going through right now. Imagine a lake. It is very turbulent and the waves are crashing into the shore.

Describe what is happening...

Finish the story on the next page…

Turbulent Waters

Then, a water turtle, who was being thrown around in the water, got an idea. He began to crash into the waves for the fun of it. He started to play in the rolling waters. Other animals joined in the fun as they felt

Pumped.

(Describe what happens next.)

ASTEROIDS

Think of the feelings you are going through right now. Tom is an astronaut out in space. He is in a little, one-man space ship trying to get out of an asteroid belt. The asteroids are crashing all around him!
Describe Tom's situation...

Finish the story on the next page...

Asteroids

Tom finally sees a clearing through the asteroid belt. He speeds up the ship and, just in the nick of time, he makes it through to the wide, open space. It was very hard for him to get through the asteroids, but now he feels

Invincible.

(Describe what happens next.)

ANT FARM

Think of the feelings you are going through right now. Imagine an ant hill. An anteater just discovered the hill and is trying to clean out all the little ants.

Describe the scene from an ant's point of view...

Finish the story on the next page...

Ant Farm

All of a sudden, a little dog notices the anteater. The dog runs toward the invader, barking and snipping at it. The anteater gets scared and scurries off into the woods. The dog returns to make sure the ants are okay. The ants feel

Trusting.

(Describe what happens next.)

AIR WAVES

Think of the feelings you are going through right now. A young eagle has decided to go flying, but it is not very skilled yet. The air is turbulent and spins the eaglet out of control. The bird doesn't know up from down.
Describe what is happening to the eagle...

Finish the story on the next page...

Air Waves

The eaglet begins to spin towards the ground, when, he throws out his wings and catches an air wave. The bird rights himself and begins to learn the way of the sky. He gradually feels more steady in the air. The eaglet is feeling

Able.
(Describe what happens next.)

STUCK IN A TREE

Think of the feelings you are going through right now. Now a kitten is high in a tree and doesn't know how to get down.

Describe what the kitten is feeling...

Finish the story on the next page…

Stuck in a Tree

A noise was heard coming closer. It was a fire engine. The truck abruptly halted in front of the tree and a fireman got out. He climbed into the basket of the fire truck and was taken up to the kitten. As he rescued the kitten, it felt

Free.

(Describe what happens next.)

THE FLOOD

Think of the feelings you are going through right now. Charlie hears the flood sirens begin to go off. He sees a large wave of water rushing his way.

Describe what Charlie goes through...

Finish the story on the next page...

The Flood

Immediately, Charlie remembers his survival skills which he had learned. He is able to get control of his situation. He then begins looking for others who were stranded in the flood. Charlie knew what to do and he felt very

Helpful.

(Describe what happens next.)

CAVE IN

Think of the feelings you are going through right now. Baby Bear is sitting in a cave when the ground begins to shake. Rocks fall over the entrance.

Describe what Baby Bear is going through...

Finish the story on the next page…

Cave In

Finally the rumbling of the mountain stopped and the dust settled. Baby Bear could see a little hole between the rocks at the entrance. He rushed over to the rocks and pulled a rock back. It moved easily. Baby Bear began to feel *Strong.*

(Describe what happens next.)

TRAPPED

Think of the feelings you are going through right now. A bunny is violently snatched up in a netted trap and cannot find a way to break free.

Describe how the bunny feels…

Finish the story on the next page…

Trapped

The bunny decided to try to chew through the net. Slowly the net began to break and soon the bunny fell to the ground and hopped away. It was feeling *Smart.*

(Describe what happens next.)

PHONE CALL

Think of the feelings you are going through right now. Jenny got a phone call. The voice on the other end gave her bad news that made her feel just like you.

Describe the phone call and how Jenny feels...

Finish the story on the next page...

Phone Call

As Jenny was thinking about how she felt, began to read a book. The book helped her to understand her situation much better and it made her feel

Informed.

(Describe what happens next.)

FALLING

Think of the feelings you are going through right now. A gosling (baby goose) was falling from its nest high on a cliff. As it fell, it kept hitting the rocks.

Describe the fall...

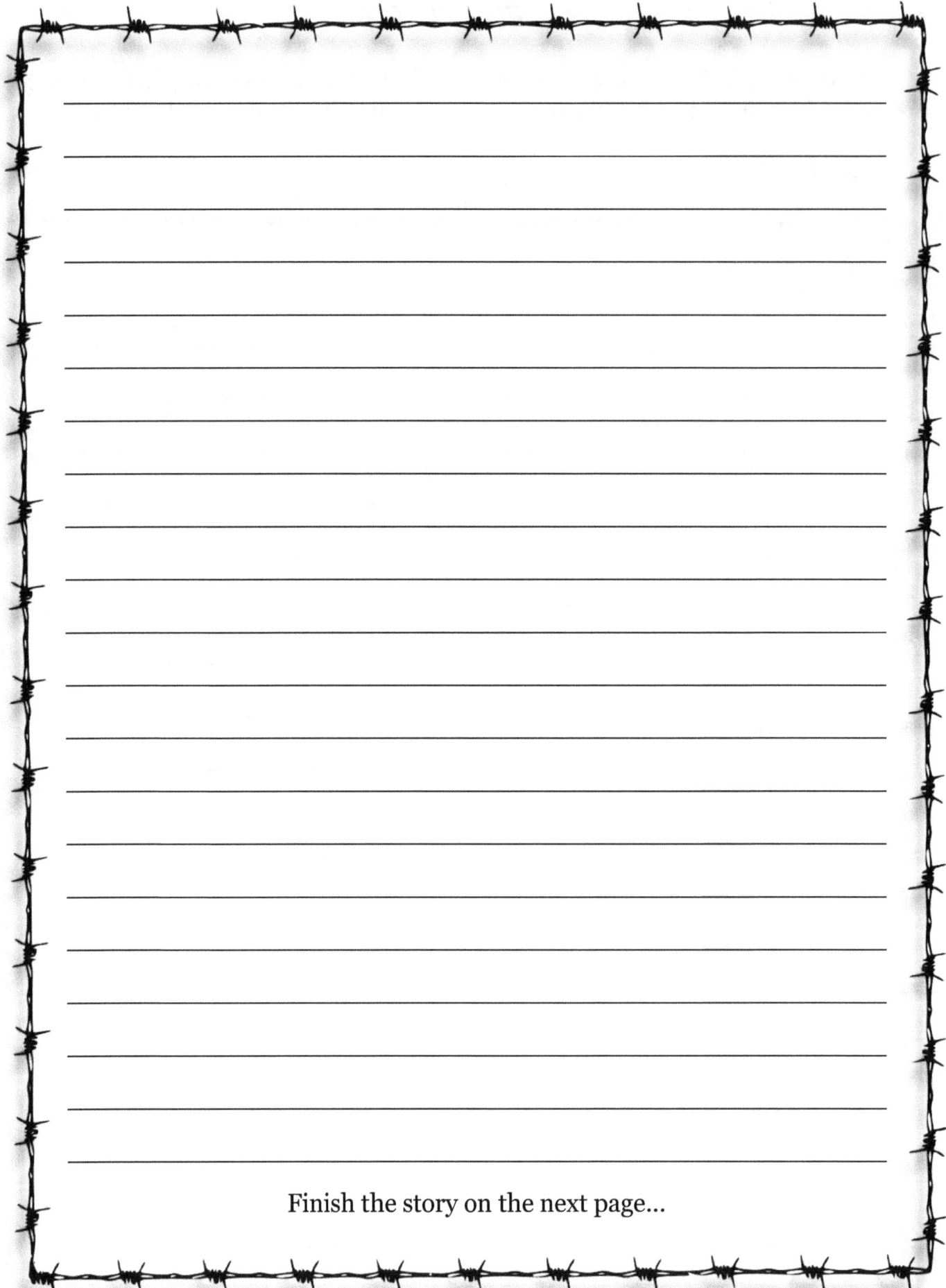

Finish the story on the next page...

Falling

Once the goose got to the bottom of cliff, its mother and father came to it to make sure it was okay. After recovering from the fall, the gosling felt

Reassured.

(Describe what happens next.)

METEOR SHOWER

Think of the feelings you are going through right now. A meteor shower is raining down large stones upon a flower garden. The flowers are being crushed.

Describe what the flowers are going through…

Finish the story on the next page...

Meteor Shower

Immediately, the meteor shower stopped and the air became still. The stones in the garden were taken away and soon all the flowers once again felt

Beautiful.

(Describe what happens next.)

THE LONE PUPPY

Think of the feelings you are going through right now. A puppy got lost in the woods and trying to find its way back home.

Describe how the potato feels...

Finish the story on the next page...

The Lone Puppy

Finally, the puppy sees a familiar path and faintly hears the sound of a boy calling for him. The voice grows louder and louder. The puppy feels *Wanted.*

(Describe what happens next.)

NOISY

Think of the feelings you are going through right now. A loud, disturbing noise is blasting through the air. Even the trees and buildings are shaking.

Describe the damage the noise is causing...

Finish the story on the next page…

Noisy

Then the noise quieted down and a little bird began to sing sweetly. The gently singing soothes the ears and the animals around now feel much more

Content.

(Describe what happens next.)

STORMY SEAS

Think of the feelings you are going through right now. Imagine a sailboat out on the ocean with a big storm all around. The boat is being tossed and turned.

Describe the scene...

Finish the story on the next page…

Stormy Seas

Suddenly, the wind dies down and ocean becomes calm. Dolphins begin to jump out of the water around the sailboat. The boat's journey is now

Easy-Going.

(Describe what happens next.)

WORMS

Think of the feelings you are going through right now. Imagine a worm that is under the ground. Rain is pouring down and destroying the ground around it.

Describe what the worm is going through…

Finish the story on the next page…

Worms

As the worm struggles, a boy bends down and picks up the worm and put it in a dry spot, out of the rain. The worm is out of danger and feels

Understood.

(Describe what happens next.)

TORNADOES

Think of the feelings you are going through right now. Imagine the wind feeling what you are feeling. It spirals into a tornado as it feels your emotions.

Describe the tornado…

Finish the story on the next page...

Tornadoes

Suddenly, the tornado hits a lake and water begins to spray around. The tornado thinks this is funny and tries to dance on the lake. It starts to feel

Spunky.

(Describe what happens next.)

SALLY

Think of the feelings you are going through right now. Sally is in her bedroom right now going feeling upset. She feels a lot like you do.

Describe Sally...

Finish the story on the next page...

Sally

Sally goes over and opens her window. As if on cue, a butterfly flits through the window and lands on the dresser. Its lovely colors lift Sally so she feels

Positive.

(Describe what happens next.)

THE TURMOIL

Think of the feelings you are going through right now. Write a story that projects your feelings into another situation or onto a particular character.

Describe that situation or what that character is going through...

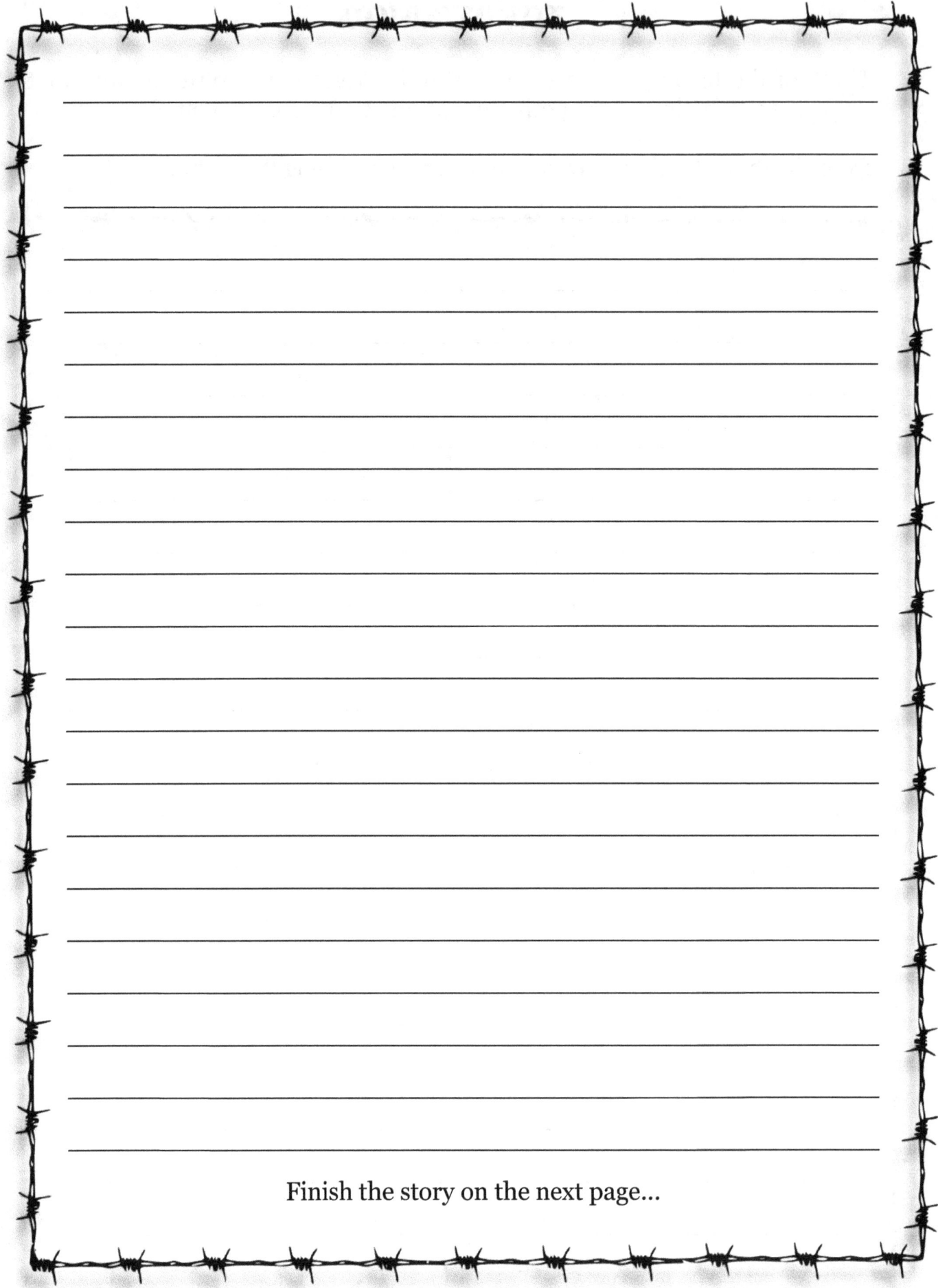

Finish the story on the next page...

Turn It Around

Complete the story by creating a something that turns the story in a different direction. Choose a positive word and move the character or situation towards that position of positivity.

(Describe what happens next.)

THE TURMOIL

Think of the feelings you are going through right now. Write a story that projects your feelings into another situation or onto a particular character.

Describe that situation or what that character is going through...

Finish the story on the next page...

Turn It Around

Complete the story by creating a something that turns the story in a different direction. Choose a positive word and move the character or situation towards that position of positivity.

(Describe what happens next.)

THE TURMOIL

Think of the feelings you are going through right now. Write a story that projects your feelings into another situation or onto a particular character.

Describe that situation or what that character is going through...

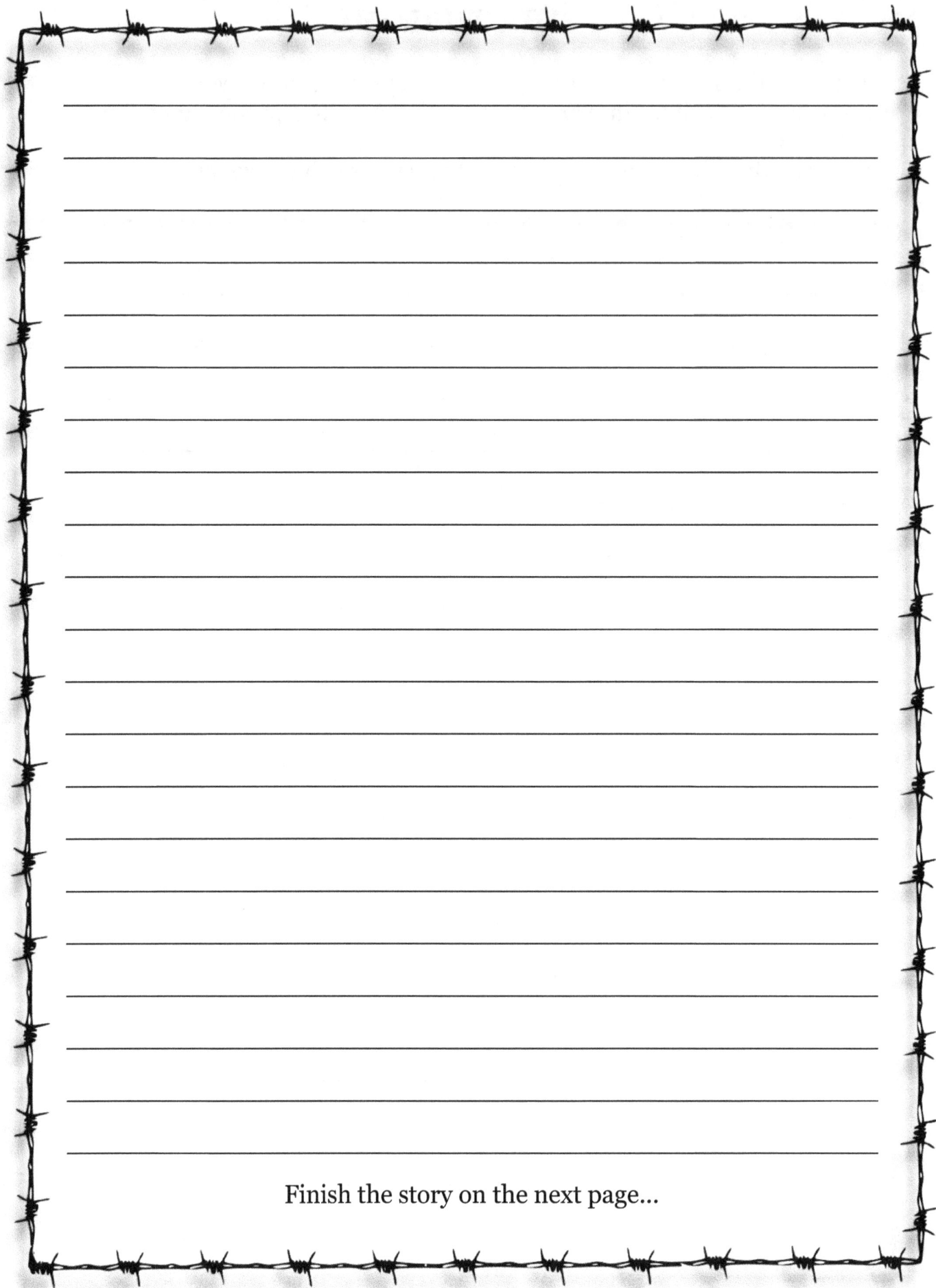

Finish the story on the next page...

Turn It Around

Complete the story by creating a something that turns the story in a different direction. Choose a positive word and move the character or situation towards that position of positivity.

(Describe what happens next.)

THE TURMOIL

Think of the feelings you are going through right now. Write a story that projects your feelings into another situation or onto a particular character.

Describe that situation or what that character is going through...

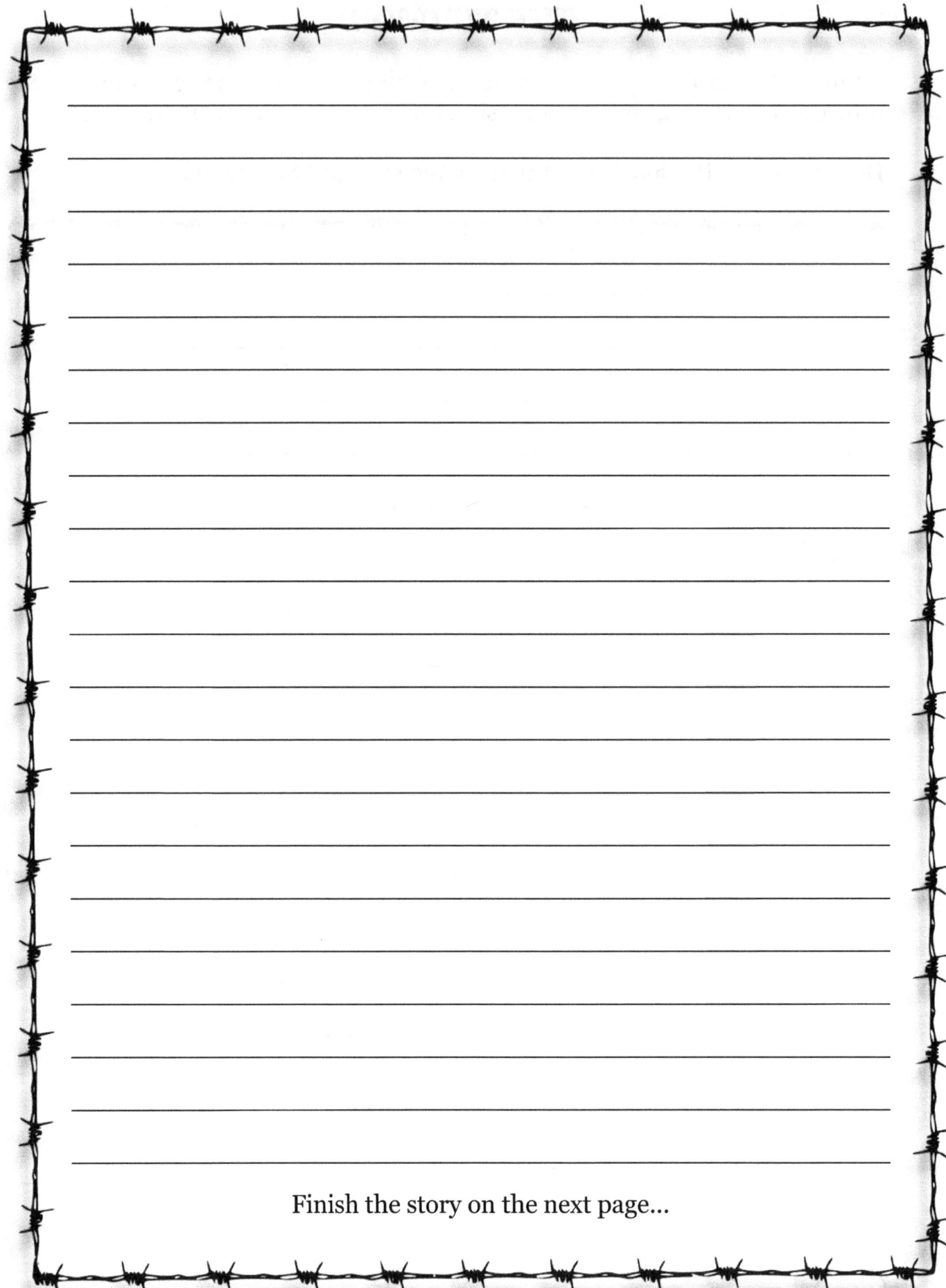

Finish the story on the next page…

Turn It Around

Complete the story by creating a something that turns the story in a different direction. Choose a positive word and move the character or situation towards that position of positivity.

(Describe what happens next.)

THE TURMOIL

Think of the feelings you are going through right now. Write a story that projects your feelings into another situation or onto a particular character.

Describe that situation or what that character is going through…

Finish the story on the next page...

Turn It Around

Complete the story by creating a something that turns the story in a different direction. Choose a positive word and move the character or situation towards that position of positivity.

(Describe what happens next.)

If you feel this book has been helpful,
please consider writing a review
and letting others know of our materials.

Thanks!

Kimberlite Kreations

KimberliteKreations.com

www.ingramcontent.com/pod-product-compliance
Lightning Source LLC
Chambersburg PA
CBHW081336080526
44588CB00017B/2639